THIS BOOK BELONGS TO

_____

The Prophets To Islam Series For Children
By Lilly S. Mohsen

This book is dedicated to all the young men who have lost their
way

May you wake up one day and realize you'll never
find true pleasure when you deviate from the right, blessed path

I know we all feel lost and blindfolded sometimes
and that's okay…

Because in my heart I also know there is a Great Lord,
Whose mercy surpasses His anger

Our Allah
If You ever see us drifting away from You…
Please bring us back
Please strengthen our weaknesses,
straighten our paths
and forgive our deepest, darkest secrets
Because my Allah, the truth is…
We are so lost without You….

Lilly S. Mohsen

The city of "Sodom" near the Dead Sea was filled with people who prayed to make-believe gods made of stone. They did all kinds of evil anyone can EVER imagine!

Most of them were groups of bullies who attacked, robbed and killed travelers.

They even found new kinds of WICKED activities to do that no other city had ever heard of before.

Allah, the One and Only God, sent a wise Prophet named Lot to the city of Sodom to teach them right from wrong.
Prophet Lot used to live in the city of Sodom, and now his job was to go back and talk to his townspeople about the Greatness and Mercy of Allah.

"My people, don't you know that evil doings upset Allah?" Prophet Lot asked them.

"Mind your own business, man!" His townspeople replied rudely.

"I can't sit back and do nothing. Oh my goodness! You've come up with WICKED activities no one has ever heard of before." Prophet Lot said sadly.

"Then leave our city if you don't like it. And if you try to stop us, we will FORCE YOU TO LEAVE!" His townspeople yelled at him.

"You're not even being good to your wives." Prophet Lot told the men. "You're all teaming up and ignoring your women. That's not very nice!"

Again, no one wanted to listen to Prophet Lot's advice

"We don't care about women. We just want to party and do nasty stuff. Mind your own business, Lot!" The men argued.

Prophet Lot was very sad. It broke his heart to watch his fellow townspeople upset Allah that way.

"Say sorry to Allah, and ask Him to forgive you. Be kind to your wives and take care of them." Prophet Lot said again and again.

"LEAVE US ALONE, LOT!" The men yelled back.

No matter what Prophet Lot said, almost no one wanted to listen to his advice.

Prophet Lot STILL never gave up!

He told his family, friends and everyone else all about Allah's mercy.

"Sorry Lot, but I don't believe in your Allah, either." Lot's wife said.

"There is only One Allah, my dear wife. Trust me, these stone gods can't help you if you're in trouble. Only Allah can." Prophet Lot explained wisely.

"Mind your own business Lot!" His wife replied rudely.

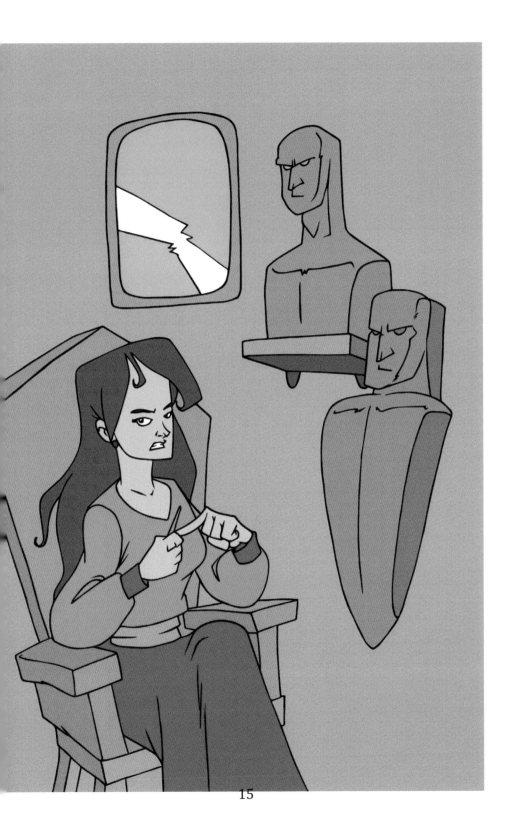

Prophet Lot's wife refused to believe in Allah, the One and Only God, but the rest of his family did. His children loved Allah so much and listened to their father.

Prophet Lot tried again.

"You rob travelers and do all kinds of evil! Aren't you scared of Allah's punishment?" Prophet Lot asked his people sadly.

"Let your Allah punish us if He could." His people mocked him. "If you're really telling the truth, then bring it on!"

Based on the meaning of Surat Al-ʿAnkabūt 29:29, Holy Qur'an

Prophet Lot was so sad.

"Oh Allah! My townspeople are not listening to my advice and they're doing so much evil." He whispered sadly. "Please help me Allah. Please help me teach them what is right from what is wrong!"

One day, two angels in the form of very handsome men came to visit Prophet Lot.

"Oh I'm worried my townspeople will try to attack you. Oh, this is going to be a hard day." Prophet Lot panicked.

"Don't worry. We came to you with a message from Allah" They both said.

"We heard you have handsome guests, Lot. Bring them out so they can join our party!" His townspeople knocked on his door loudly.

"Please don't embarrass me. These are my guests. Please treat them kindly and with respect." Prophet Lot tried to reason with his townspeople.

"We will treat them any way we want. BRING THEM OUT!" They yelled.

"Don't worry." One of Prophet Lot's visitors said, "Allah sent us to you. Your people can't harm you or your family. Just wait till nighttime falls then take your family and leave. Leave the city and don't look back. Your wife won't come with you. She will be struck by what will strike your people in the morning. Isn't the morning coming soon?"

Based on meaning of Surat Hud 11:81, Holy Qur'an

The next morning, Allah ordered one of His angels to flip the city of 'Sodom' upside down and ordered the sky to pour down stones of hard clay.

Allah doesn't like those who spread evil and He certainly doesn't like bullies.

Prophet Lot and his family were saved, all except his evil wife.

The city of Sodom was destroyed, while Prophet Lot and his followers lived happily ever after.

The End

Printed in Great Britain
by Amazon